VOTE
VOTE
VOTE
AF584451

THE PRIME MINISTER

John Lesley

REDBACK publishing

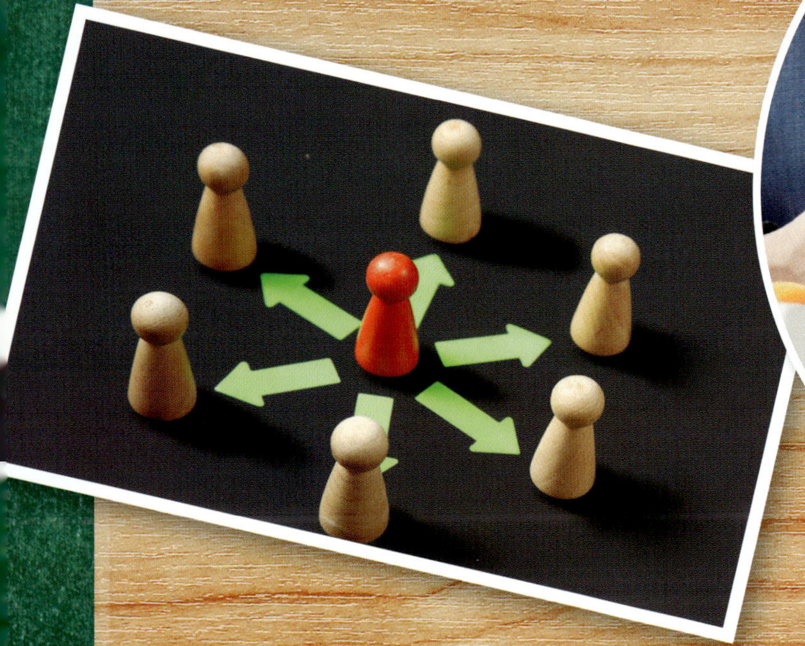

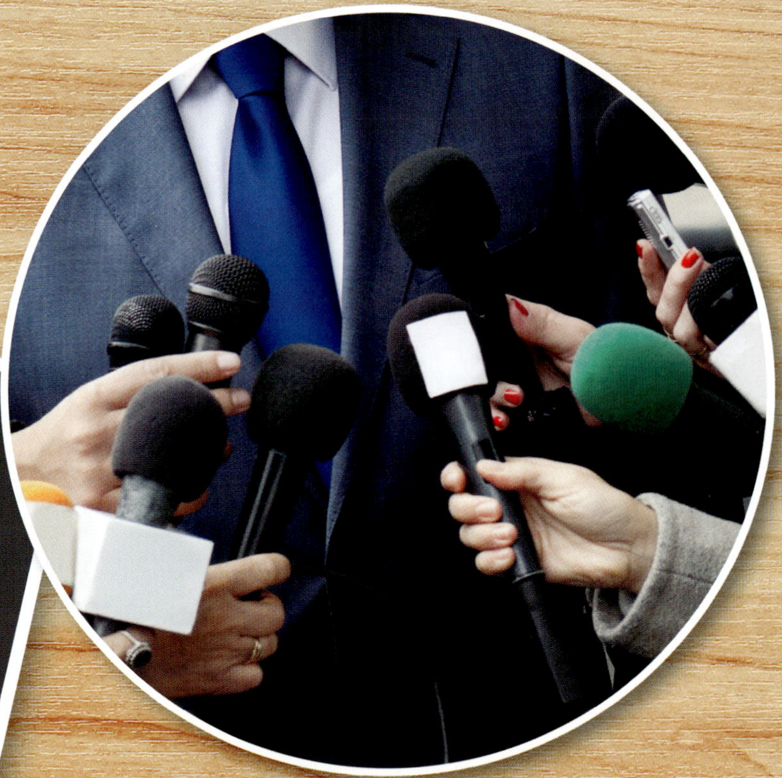

First Published 2026 by
Redback Publishing
Suite 6, 13a Narabang Way,
Belrose NSW 2085
Australia

www.redbackpublishing.com
orders@redbackpublishing.com

ISBN 978-1-761401-13-8

Author: John Lesley
Editor: Caroline Thomas
Designer: Redback Publishing

Original illustrations © Redback Publishing 2026
Originated by Redback Publishing

A catalogue record for this book is available from the National Library of Australia

CONTENTS

THE PRIME MINISTER

The Prime Minister is the leader of the political party that forms the Government after an election.

Surprisingly, the position of Prime Minister is not described in the Constitution, and exists instead through tradition. The British Parliament had a Prime Minister, so it followed naturally that after Federation, in 1901, the new Australian Commonwealth would have one too.

If the Prime Minister is ill or away visiting another country, the deputy leader of his political party usually becomes the Acting Prime Minister. If the Liberal Party/Nationals coalition has formed the Government, then the leader of the Nationals automatically becomes the Acting Prime Minister if the Prime Minister is away.
The Prime Minister is usually a member of the House of Representatives.

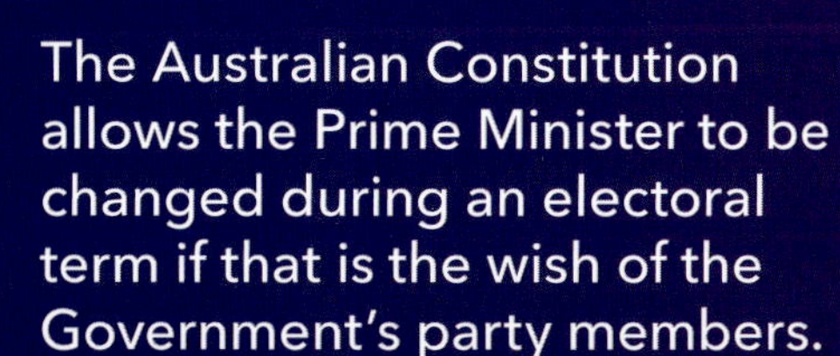

The Australian Constitution allows the Prime Minister to be changed during an electoral term if that is the wish of the Government's party members.

WHAT DOES THE PRIME MINISTER DO?

 Oversees Government policies and law-making	 Chooses and removes Ministers	 Heads the Cabinet
 Is a member of the Executive Council	 Has ultimate responsibility for Government actions	 Nominates a person to be the new Governor-General
 Represents Australia on overseas visits and at meetings	 Represents the Government at community and social events	 Maintains contact with their own electorate and the voters

	Is present at Question Time in Parliament to answer any questions	Presents various Prime Minister's awards for outstanding contributions to society by citizens and groups	Holds party meetings to discuss policies
	Sets the date for the next Federal election and asks the Governor-General to dissolve Parliament so that a new election can take place at least every three years		Takes the Oath of Office or Affirmation of Office (depending on religious preference) before officially becoming the Prime Minister, swearing to serve the people and the Monarch
		Campaigns during an election campaign to promote their own party as the best choice for forming a reliable and trustworthy government	

WHO CHOOSES THE PRIME MINISTER?

A Prime Minister is elected by their own party by methods that the party itself decides. The Liberal Party and The Nationals coalition always has the Liberal Party leader as Prime Minister when they are forming the Government. All Liberal Party members who have been elected to Parliament can vote for their leader.

If the Australian Labor Party is forming Government, their leader, and therefore the Prime Minister, is chosen by a combined vote by party members elected to Parliament as well as by non-elected party members.

By tradition, the Prime Minister is a Member of the House of Representatives, not of the Senate.

Prime Minister John Gorton was a Senator when elected to the position in 1968, but within weeks he resigned from the Senate and won a by-election that was being held for a seat in the House of Representatives.

John Gorton

SWEARING-IN

The Prime Minister is not officially able to hold that office until being sworn in by the Governor-General. It is an accepted convention that the person sworn in as Prime Minister will be the leader of the Parliamentary Party that has the most elected members in the House of Representatives. However, this requirement is not specified in the Australian Constitution, which makes no mention of the position of Prime Minister at all.

Gough Whitlam

REMOVING A PRIME MINISTER

A Prime Minister can be removed from office if their political party votes and chooses another leader. At the end of the Government's term, which is three years, the Governor-General dissolves Parliament and calls an election. This removes the whole Government from power, including the Prime Minister.

The Governor-General can also dissolve Parliament and remove the Prime Minister in the middle of the three-year term. This happened in 1975 when the Governor-General dismissed the Prime Minster, Gough Whitlam.

THE PM CHOOSES MINISTERS

A Minister is an elected member of the Government who has been given special responsibilities by the Prime Minister. These responsibilities are called a portfolio, and they are managed by a Department or other bureaucratic body under the control of the Minister. Departments are the main way that Government policies are put into action through work done by public servants. Examples of portfolios include health, defence, finance, trade, and education.

MEDICARE

Ministers can be chosen from Government members in either the House of Representatives or the Senate.

CABINET

Ministers who have the most important responsibilities are known as senior Ministers. Together, the senior Ministers and the Prime Minister form the Cabinet. The Cabinet is responsible for all major Government decisions.

It is essential for Cabinet members to be able to speak freely and explore all options, before making very important decisions that affect the Australian public. To allow this, the recordings of Cabinet meetings are kept secret for twenty years.

ASSISTANT MINISTER

An Assistant Minister is a person who assists a Minister to run their department. They are chosen from the Government members in either House of Parliament, and they used to be called Parliamentary Secretaries.

SHADOW MINISTERS

Shadow Ministers are selected by the Leader of the Opposition. A Government Minister may have a Shadow Minister who closely follows everything they do, and points out any negative aspects of their policies. The Shadow Cabinet consists of the Leader of the Opposition party and all of its Ministers that shadow the Government Ministers. The Shadow Cabinet plans the laws it would introduce if its party were to become the Government at the next Federal election.

EXECUTIVE COUNCIL

SEPARATION OF POWERS

The Executive Council is a branch of government that forms one of the three sections that provide for the Separation of Powers. It is similar in nature to the Privy Council in Britain.

The Separation of Powers reduces the likelihood of any one section of government gaining absolute power over Australia. Each branch operates mostly independently of the other and cannot be directed on what decisions to make. All three sections are expected to follow the rules laid down in the Australian Constitution.

The Separation of Powers three sections are:

1. **The Australian Parliament**

2. **The Executive**

3. **The Judiciary**

The Executive Council is made up of the Governor-General, the Prime Minister and Ministers, both current and past. Appointment of a Minister to the Executive Council is for life, and remains in place even when the Minister no longer sits in Parliament. The Governor-General has the power to remove a Councillor for misconduct.

William Hughes was the oldest person to serve on the Executive Council, at 90 years old.

Ministers appointed to the Executive Council have the formal title 'The Honourable' added before their name. This title can remain with them for life, even after they have left Parliament.

In practice, it is the Cabinet that makes the decisions, and the Executive Council that is the Cabinet's legal basis for power. The Executive Council is engaged in the formal procedures which accompany the signing of important documents. Its members, except for the Governor-General, are called Executive Councillors.

THE BENCHES

FRONTBENCHERS

Frontbenchers are Ministers and Shadow Ministers. They sit in the front rows of whichever side of Parliament their party occupies. In the House of Representatives, they sit directly behind either the Prime Minister or the Leader of the Opposition. Frontbenchers can be in either House of Parliament.

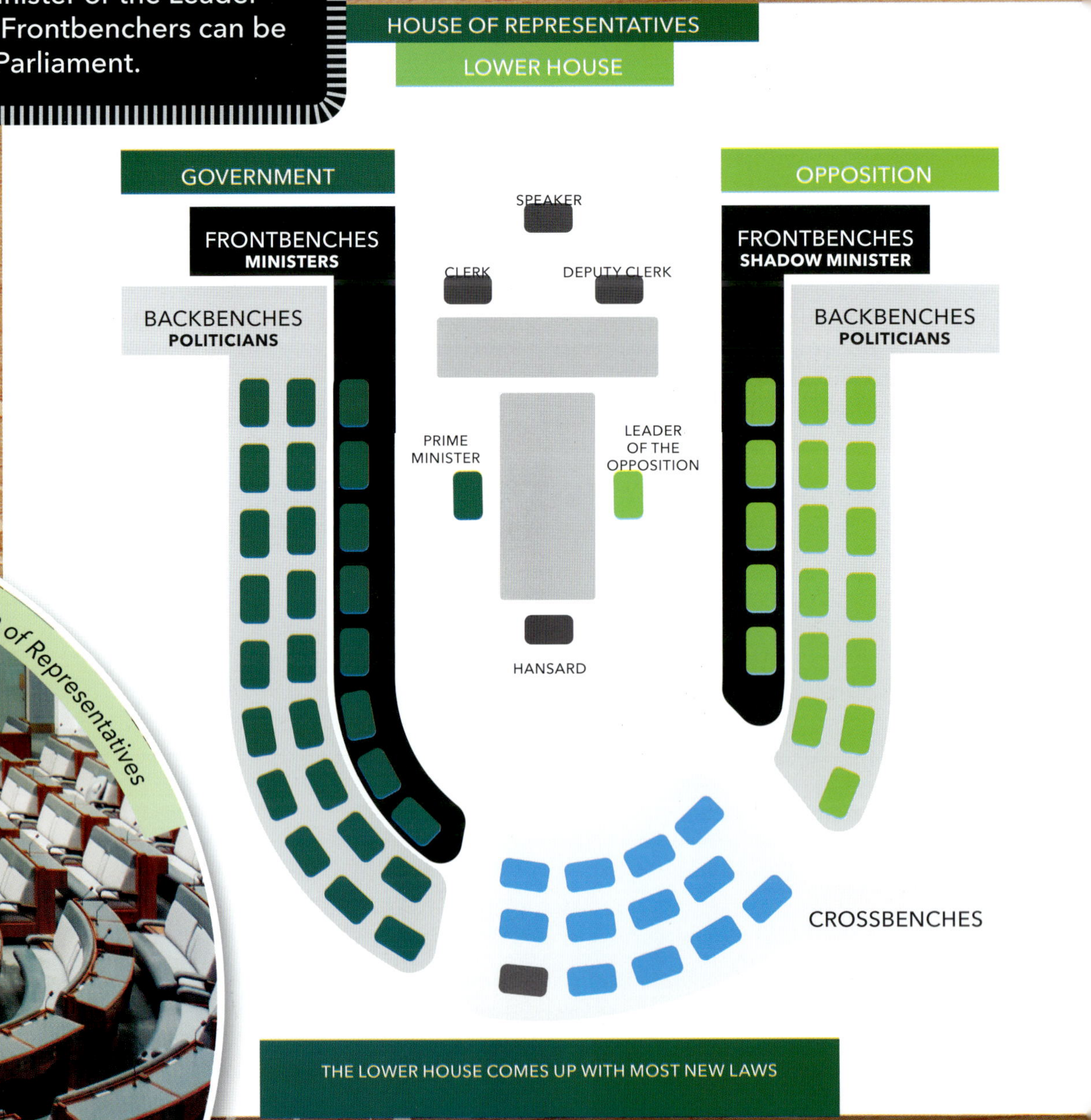

HOUSE OF REPRESENTATIVES

LOWER HOUSE

GOVERNMENT

OPPOSITION

SPEAKER

FRONTBENCHES
MINISTERS

FRONTBENCHES
SHADOW MINISTER

CLERK

DEPUTY CLERK

BACKBENCHES
POLITICIANS

BACKBENCHES
POLITICIANS

PRIME MINISTER

LEADER OF THE OPPOSITION

HANSARD

CROSSBENCHES

THE LOWER HOUSE COMES UP WITH MOST NEW LAWS

The House of Representatives

BACKBENCHERS

Backbenchers are the elected politicians who do not have a major portfolio. They sit at the back of the rows of seats in the House of Parliament to which they were elected. They spend time looking after the needs of their electorate, and they bring matters to the attention of Parliament that would not otherwise have any chance of having such public exposure. Backbenchers take part in debates about the Bills that are introduced into Parliament.

Senate - Upper House

SENATE

UPPER HOUSE

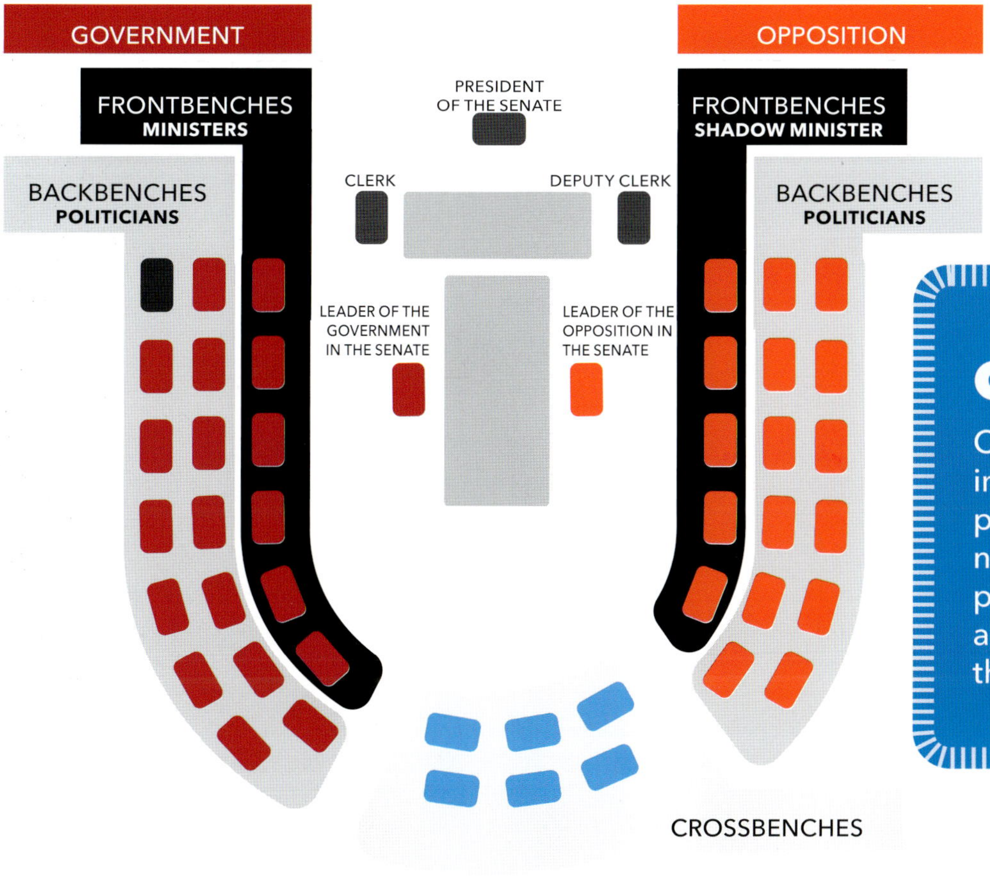

GOVERNMENT

FRONTBENCHES
MINISTERS

BACKBENCHES
POLITICIANS

PRESIDENT OF THE SENATE

CLERK

DEPUTY CLERK

LEADER OF THE GOVERNMENT IN THE SENATE

LEADER OF THE OPPOSITION IN THE SENATE

OPPOSITION

FRONTBENCHES
SHADOW MINISTER

BACKBENCHES
POLITICIANS

CROSSBENCHES

THE SENATE CHECKS NEW LAWS

CROSSBENCHES

Crossbenches are the seats in Parliament where elected politicians sit who are not members of the main parliamentary parties. They are in the curved section of the seating.

THE OPPOSITION

The Leader of the Opposition is an important role in the Westminster System of government. The position is held by the leader of the second-largest political party elected to Parliament and it involves leading the Opposition's criticism of Government policies and decisions.

The Leader of the Opposition and the Prime Minister sit face-to-face in the House of Representatives in Parliament House. The two leaders often have heated debates over proposed legislation. While these are the moments that tend to be reported most often by news services, the work of the Parliament is not always so fiery. Legislation that is approved by both sides of Parliament often passes with no changes or with minor amendments and with little need for extensive debate.

The Opposition chooses Shadow Ministers who question the actions of the Ministers of the Government.

AMERICAN INFLUENCE

PRIME MINISTER OR PRESIDENT?

Before Federation in 1901, some Australian colonies discussed adopting a federal democratic republic form of government such as is used in the USA. Some groups hoped for Australia to become a republic, like the American colonies had, but the lack of a strong local defence force made many people uneasy. They believed they would have to rely on Britain to rescue them if Australia were ever invaded by a foreign power.

The presidential style of government used in the United States did become an alternative model of the Westminster System in some countries, but the new Commonwealth of Australia still had strong ties with Britain. This connection led to the system of Government that we still use today. We have a Prime Minister as the leader of the Government, and a Governor-General who represents the Monarch. The Governor-General is both the Head of State and the Commander-in-Chief of the Australian Defence Force.

In the USA, the President has more power than a Prime Minister, since a President holds all the three roles of leader of Government, Head of State and Commander-in-Chief of the military.

In Australia, you will hear the term 'President' used to refer to the President of the Senate. This role is not similar to that of the President of the USA, and it simply refers to the person who ensures order is maintained in Senate procedures.

OFFICIAL RESIDENCES

The Prime Minister has two official residences in Australia. They are both heritage-listed buildings that combine the functions of family homes, as well as places to host official events and hold meetings. They are large houses rather than formal mansions in the style of the country mansions of Britain.

KIRRIBILLI HOUSE, SYDNEY

While in Sydney, the Prime Minister stays at Kirribilli House. It was built in 1854 and acquired by the Australian government in 1920. After being used for a variety of government purposes, in the 1950s Kirribilli House became one of the Prime Minister's official residences.

THE LODGE, CANBERRA

In Canberra, the Prime Minister lives at The Lodge. It was built as an official residence in the 1920s and was supposed to be only a temporary choice for that purpose. Despite this, it is still being used a century later.

Constant work is needed to keep the buildings suitable for their roles. For example, it is essential that the Australian Prime Minister has a safe place to live. High levels of security must always be in force at both residences. This is one of the reasons that a Prime Minister resides at the official residences.

WORKING FOR THE PRIME MINISTER

People who are interested in the way government functions in Australia might consider working in the Department of Prime Minister and Cabinet. As with all public servants, employees are expected to help enable the current Government's policies, and to perform their duties without personal bias and to a very high standard.

The Prime Minister of Australia works from their office in Parliament House, their office in their electorate, the floor of the House of Representatives, and many other locations.

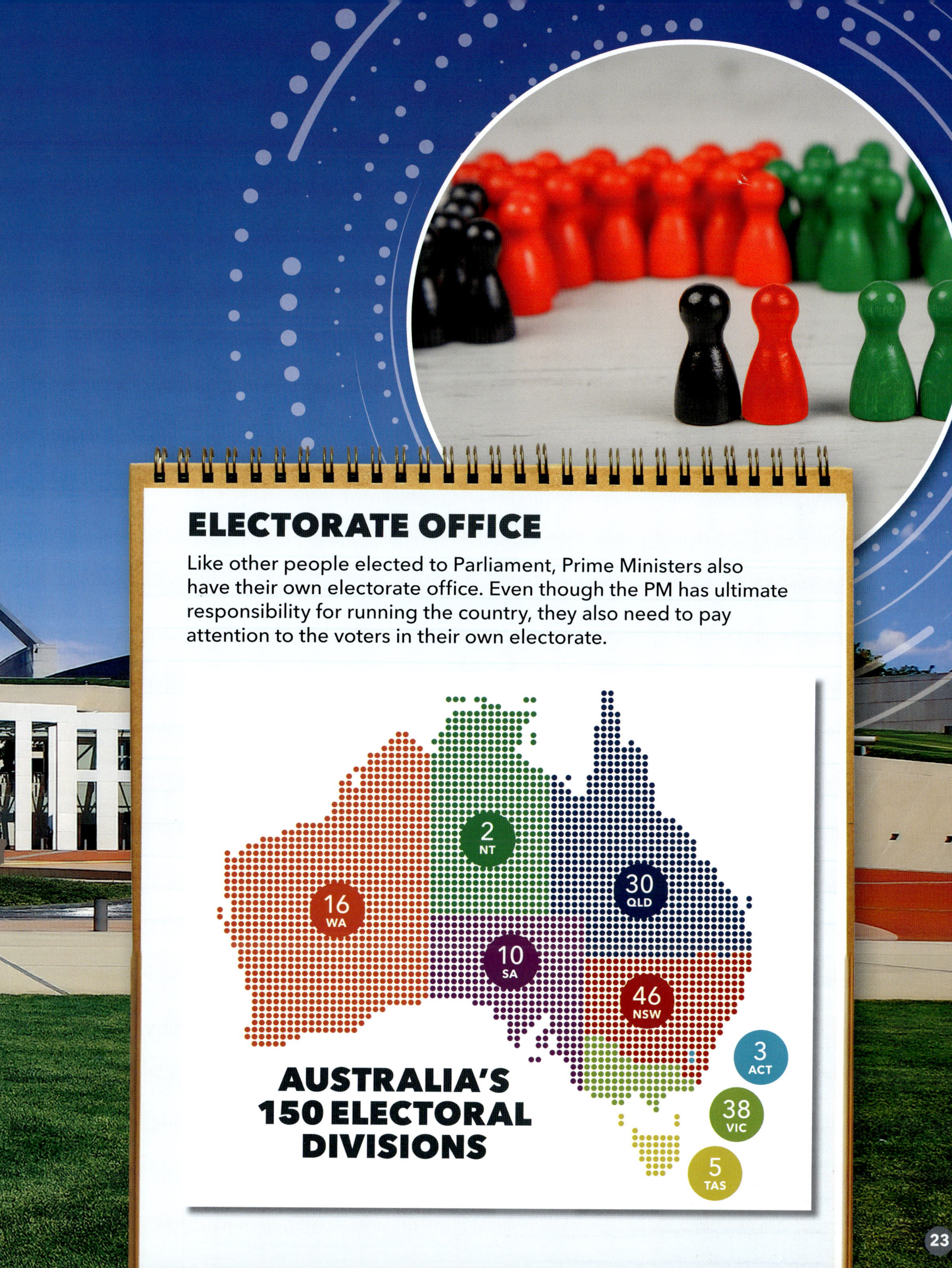

ELECTORATE OFFICE

Like other people elected to Parliament, Prime Ministers also have their own electorate office. Even though the PM has ultimate responsibility for running the country, they also need to pay attention to the voters in their own electorate.

TRAVEL

The Prime Minister of Australia is expected to travel overseas, representing Australia and its interests. They also travel internally, meeting with people and promoting the Government's policies. Senior Ministers also travel for the same purposes.

REASONS FOR OVERSEAS TRAVEL INCLUDE:

- Negotiating better trade deals for Australian farmers
- Looking after the rights of Australian citizens overseas
- Presenting Australia's viewpoints at international meetings
- Promoting Australian industry overseas
- Attending funerals and weddings of important political leaders or members of the Royal Family
- Discussing Australia's security with allies overseas
- Forging new alliances overseas

REASONS FOR TRAVEL WITHIN AUSTRALIA INCLUDE:

- Visiting disaster zones in Australia to provide moral support
- Discussing key Government policies with the public to ensure they understand the facts
- Campaigning for an upcoming election

The PM may use RAAF aircraft when travelling

PRIME MINISTERS SINCE 1901

Since Federation in 1901, Australia has had 31 Prime Ministers, with some of them serving more than one term in that position.

1 Edmund Barton

1901-03

2 Alfred Deakin

1903-1904; 1905-1908; 1909-1910

3 John Christian Watson

1904

4 George Houston Reid

1904-05

5 Andrew Fisher

1908-09; 1910-13; 1914-15

6 Joseph Cook

1913-14

7 William Morris Hughes

1915-23

8 Stanley Melbourne Bruce

1923-29

9 James Henry Scullin

1929-32

10 Joseph Aloysius Lyons

1932-39

11 Earle Christmas Grafton Page

1939

12 Robert Gordon Menzies

1939-41; 1949-66

13 Arthur William Fadden

1941

14 John Curtin

1941-45

15 Francis Michael Forde

1945

16

Joseph Benedict Chifley
1945-49

17

Harold Edward Holt
1966-67

18

John McEwen
1967-68

19

John Grey Gorton
1968-71

20

William McMahon
1971-72

21

Edward Gough Whitlam
1972-75

22

John Malcolm Fraser
1975-83

23

Robert James Lee Hawke
1983-91

24

Paul John Keating
1991-96

25

John Winston Howard
1996-2007

26

Kevin Michael Rudd
2007-10; 2013

27

Julia Eileen Gillard
2010-13

28

Anthony John Abbott
2013-15

29

Malcolm Bligh Turnbull
2015-2018

30

Scott John Morrison
2018-2022

31

Anthony Norman Albanese
2022-

NOTABLE PRIME MINISTERS

AUSTRALIA'S FIRST PM, EDMUND BARTON

Edmund Barton was born in Sydney in 1849. He was a member of the New South Wales Parliament and played a leading role in the Federation of the colonies of Australia to form the Commonwealth of Australia. He was sworn in as Prime Minister by Australia's first Governor-General, Lord Hopetoun, on 1 January 1901. On 9 March 1901, the first Federal election was held, and Barton remained Prime Minister. He retired from Parliament in 1903 to become a Justice of the High Court of Australia.

AUSTRALIA'S LONGEST-SERVING PM, SIR ROBERT MENZIES

Robert Gordon Menzies was Prime Minister of Australia twice. He was born in country Victoria and studied law at university. He entered Parliament in 1934 as a member of the United Australia Party. Menzies became leader of the party and Prime Minister in 1939. The party forced him to resign in 1941. He went on to form and lead the Liberal Party in 1944 and again became Prime Minister at the Federal election in 1949 (in coalition with the Country Party). He remained Prime Minister for eighteen years.

SACKED PM, GOUGH WHITLAM

Edward Gough Whitlam was born in Melbourne in 1916. He studied law at Sydney University and became a Labor MP in the 1952 Federal election. He became deputy leader of the Labor Party in 1960 and leader in 1967. He was Leader of the Opposition until the Labor Party won the 1972 election. Whitlam then became the first Labor Prime Minister in 23 years. When Whitlam became Prime Minister, Australian soldiers were fighting a war in Vietnam. Whitlam's Government ended Australia's part in that war. After some of the Bills passed in the House of Representatives were repeatedly rejected by the Senate, the Governor-General, Sir John Kerr, sacked Gough Whitlam and his Labor Government. Sir John Kerr appointed the Leader of the Opposition, Malcolm Fraser, as caretaker Prime Minister until an election six weeks later. Gough Whitlam remained leader of the Opposition until 1978 when he retired from Parliament.

AUSTRALIA'S FIRST FEMALE PM, JULIA GILLARD

On 24 June 2010, Julia Gillard became Australia's first female Prime Minister. Born in 1961 in Wales, her family migrated to Australia in 1966. She was the Federal Member for Labor (Vic) and was first elected to Parliament in 1998. She served as Deputy Prime Minister from 2007 to 2010 and became Prime Minister after a leadership challenge, which saw Prime Minister Kevin Rudd stand down. One month later, she called an election, which Labor won by forming a coalition with the Greens and three Independents. On 26 June 2013, Julia Gillard was defeated in a leadership ballot by Kevin Rudd, who was sworn in as Prime Minister the following day. Soon after, she retired from politics.

FAST FACTS ABOUT THE PM

31

Thirty-one people have held the position of PM.

There has been one female PM, Julia Gillard.

The PM is chosen by their party, not elected by the people.

The spouse or partner of the PM does not have any special title in Australia.

Robert Menzies served as PM for eighteen years, the longest term so far.

The youngest PM was John Watson, who was thirty-seven years old when he became PM in 1904.

The position of PM is not mentioned in the Constitution.

GLOSSARY

allies .... countries that can be relied upon for help during war

amendments .... official changes to laws

bias .... prejudice

campaign (verb) .... promote a set of policies in preparation for an election

heritage (adjective) .... relating to historical significance

legislation .... laws

negotiate .... discuss and compromise

nominate .... name a person for a special role

portfolio .... set of responsibilities that come with being a Minister in Parliament

public servant .... person who is employed by the government

residence .... place where a person has their home

swear-in .... officially install a person in a position after they take an oath

term .... period during which a Government can be in power before having to face another election

tradition .... actions that are based on the way things were done in the past

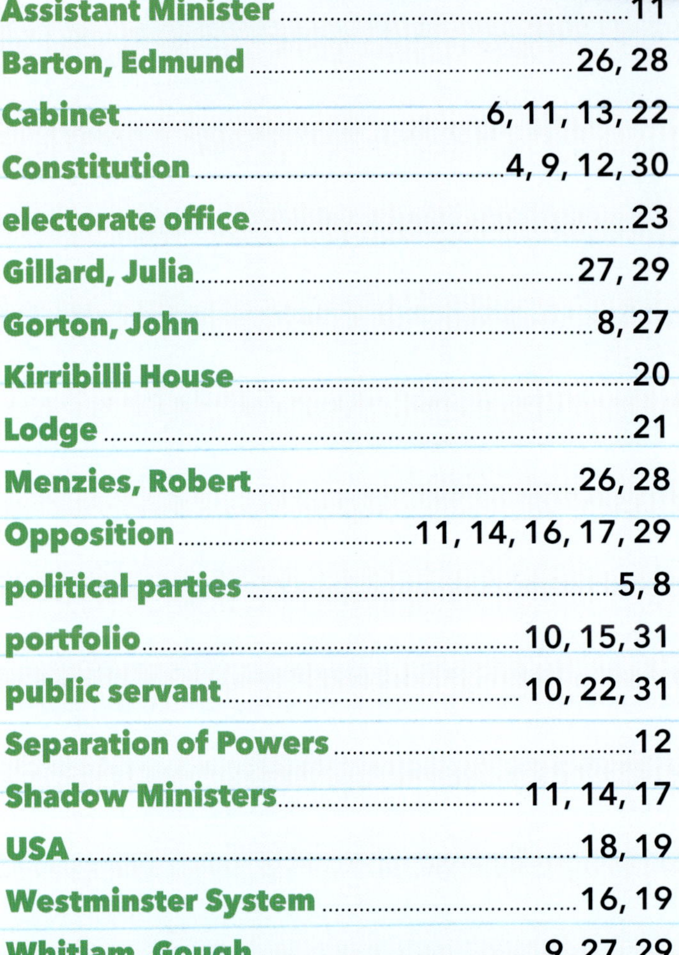

INDEX

Acknowledgements

Abbreviations: l–left, r–right, b–bottom, t–top, c–centre, m–middle

We would like to thank the following for permission to reproduce photographs (images © Shutterstock unless otherwise stated): Pg3br LemonMyrtle / Shutterstock.com, pg8mr National Archives of Australia, Public domain, via Wikimedia Commons, pg9bl Australian Conservation Foundation, CC BY-SA 4.0 <https://creativecommons.org/licenses/by-sa/4.0>, via Wikimedia Commons, pg10bl Ryan Fletcher / Shutterstock.com, pg13tr National Library of Australia, pg13b Argus (Melbourne, Vic.)(Life time: N/A), Public domain, via Wikimedia Commons, pg19mr Rawpixel.com / Shutterstock.com, pg13b katacarix / Shutterstock.com, pg20t Sardaka (talk) 07:47, 18 September 2013 (UTC), CC BY 3.0 <https://creativecommons.org/licenses/by/3.0>, via Wikimedia Commons, pg20bl LemonMyrtle / Shutterstock.com, pg21t © Commonwealth of Australia 2016, CC BY-SA 4.0 <https://creativecommons.org/licenses/by-sa/4.0>, via Wikimedia Commons, pg21br IOIO IMAGES / Shutterstock.com, pg22bl ChameleonsEye / Shutterstock.com, pg24-25m Bidgee, CC BY-SA 3.0 AU <https://creativecommons.org/licenses/by-sa/3.0/au/deed.en>, via Wikimedia Commons, pg26 1: State Library of Queensland, 3: National Library of Australia, Public domain, via Wikimedia Commons, 4: See page for author, Public domain, via Wikimedia Commons, 5: National Library of Australia, Public domain, via Wikimedia Commons, 6: Crown Studios, Public domain, via Wikimedia Commons, 7: National Library of Australia, Public domain, via Wikimedia Commons, 8: Fairfax archive of glass plate negatives, Public domain, via Wikimedia Commons, 9: National Library of Australia, Public domain, via Wikimedia Commons, 10: not specified, Public domain, via Wikimedia Commons, 11: Falk Studios, Public domain, via Wikimedia Commons, 12: Luke Monte, Public domain, via Wikimedia Commons, 13: National Library of Australia, Public domain, via Wikimedia Commons, 14: National Library of Australia, Public domain, via Wikimedia Commons, 15: Government of Australia: Department of Information, Public domain, via Wikimedia Commons, 16: Contributor(s): Queensland Newspapers Pty Ltd, Public domain, via Wikimedia Commons, 17: Commonwealth Parliamentary Library official photograph – National Library of Australia, Public domain, via Wikimedia Commons, 18: National Library of Australia, Public domain, via Wikimedia Commons, 19: Australian Information Service, Public domain, via Wikimedia Commons, 20: Australian News and Information Bureau, Public domain, via Wikimedia Commons, 21: National Archives of Australia, Public domain, via Wikimedia Commons, 22: National Archives of Australia, CC BY 3.0 AU <https://creativecommons.org/licenses/by/3.0/au/deed.en>, via Wikimedia Commons, 23: © Commonwealth of Australia 2011, CC BY-SA 3.0 AU <https://creativecommons.org/licenses/by-sa/3.0/au/deed.en>, via Wikimedia Commons, 24: © Commonwealth of Australia 2011, CC BY-SA 3.0 <https://creativecommons.org/licenses/by-sa/3.0>, via Wikimedia Commons, 25: © Commonwealth of Australia 2011, CC BY-SA 3.0 <https://creativecommons.org/licenses/by-sa/3.0>, via Wikimedia Commons, 26: Department of Foreign Affairs and Trade website – www.dfat.gov.au, CC BY 4.0 <https://creativecommons.org/licenses/by/4.0>, via Wikimedia Commons, 27: Dilma Rousseff, CC BY-SA 2.0 <https://creativecommons.org/licenses/by-sa/2.0>, via Wikimedia Commons, 28: Tony Abbott, CC BY 2.0 <https://creativecommons.org/licenses/by/2.0>, via Wikimedia Commons, 29: Commonwealth of Australia, CC BY 3.0 AU <https://creativecommons.org/licenses/by/3.0/au/deed.en>, via Wikimedia Commons, 30: Department of Prime Minister and Cabinet, CC BY 3.0 AU <https://creativecommons.org/licenses/by/3.0/au/deed.en>, via Wikimedia Commons, 31: Australian Government, CC BY 4.0 <https://creativecommons.org/licenses/by/4.0>, via Wikimedia Commons, pg28tr State Library of New South Wales P1/126., Public domain, via Wikimedia Commons, pg28bl National Library of Australia, Public domain, via Wikimedia Commons, pg29tr Work of the Australian Government, Public domain, via Wikimedia Commons, pg29bl MystifyMe Concert Photography (Troy), CC BY 2.0 <https://creativecommons.org/licenses/by/2.0>, via Wikimedia Commons, pg30tr Featureflash Photo Agency / Shutterstock.com, pg30bl National Library of Australia, Public domain, via Wikimedia Commons John Watson, pg30 Steve Tritton / Shutterstock.com, pg32tr Bidgee, CC BY-SA 3.0 AU <https://creativecommons.org/licenses/by-sa/3.0/au/deed.en>, via Wikimedia Commons

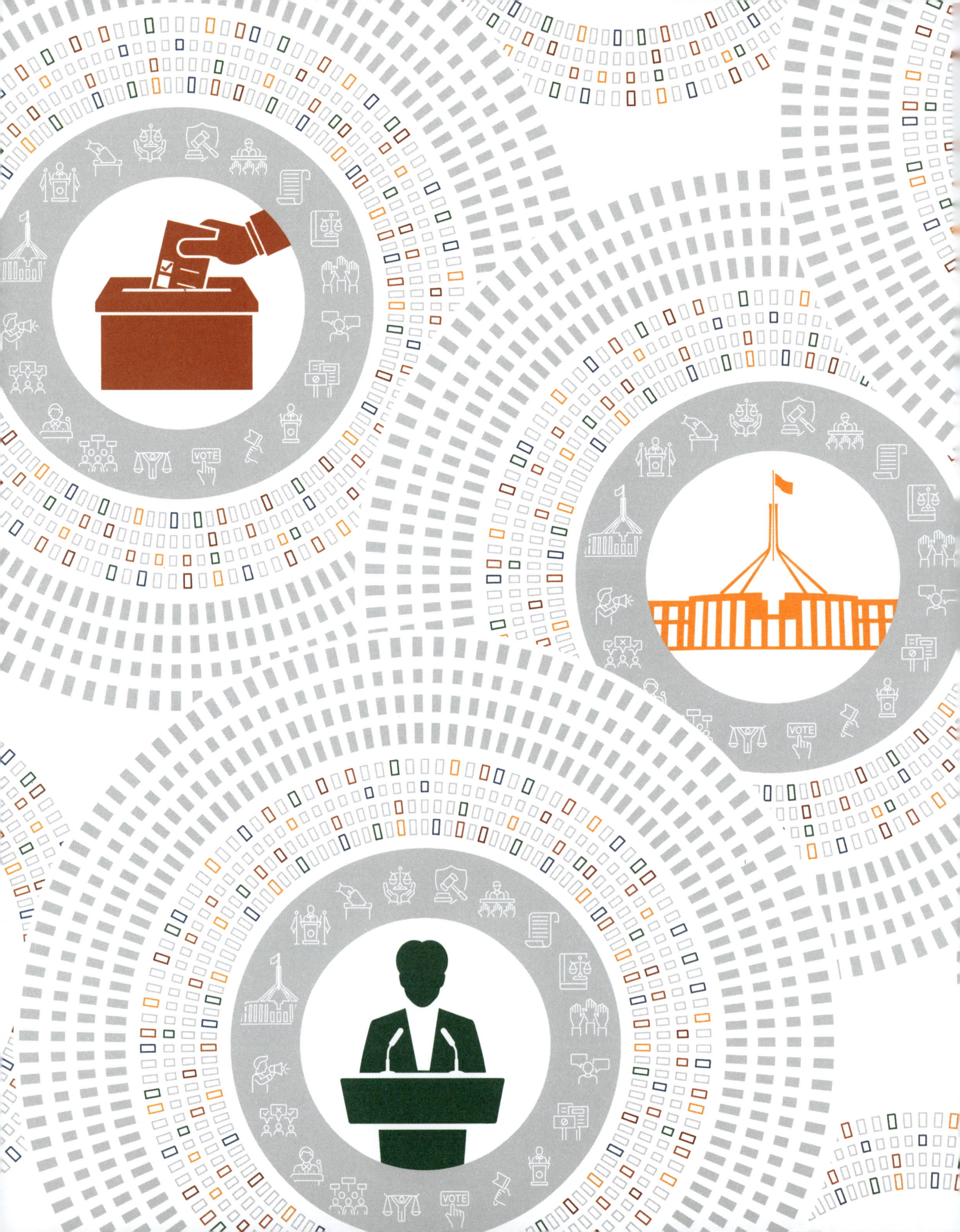
VOTE
VOTE
VOTE